Obstacles

5 Life Lessons to Be Successful In The Real World

by:

Jason Judkins

ISBN-10: 1500931462
ISBN-13: 978-1500931462

About The Author

Follow Me On:

Facebook:

http://www.facebook.com/ASecretLie

On Twitter:

http://www.twitter.com/ASecretLie

Email: asecretlie@gmail.com

If you like this book, check out my other books!

"A Secret Lie: How The World Really Is:"
http://www.amazon.com/dp/B007P5CJKM

"CREATE Your Way Out Of DEBT"
http://www.amazon.com/dp/B00LGX57J4

"How Ta Get PU$$Y"
http://www.amazon.com/dp/B00L0LZC6U

Check out my newest film about how the world really is:

https://www.createspace.com/403985

Check out my NEW Audiobooks for FREE at:

on Relationships:
http://open.spotify.com/album/64vuXdOD
VyppQcsrX807M5

on Religion:
http://open.spotify.com/album/0SY2Wtr5jn
UouXGeboSVNO

Like to Laugh? Click this link to see the funniest, just released, stand-up comedy FREE!

http://open.spotify.com/album/2S65s3bo
HGcsDzZIUwy8aO

For the Best Alternative Rock Music, click below!
http://open.spotify.com/album/7A1p0qBw3oov8b
KYsA26Aw

This book is dedicated to fighting corruption and inequality in all forms at all levels, and also to challenge conventional thinking.

Contents

CONTENTS (CONTINUED)

Advisory

The author of this book, Jason Judkins, is not a licensed professional in the subject matter covered. The contents are opinion and based on the author's life experience. The author assumes no liability or responsibility from the consequences of reading this book! This book has mature language.

Preface

People always ask, where do I get my inspiration from. The idea first came about five years ago. A middle-aged women I knew, with two kids, suddenly died in a car wreck. I thought, what if that suddenly happened to me? I have kids of my own. How would they learn about life? Who would teach them? How would they know their dad's views on things? There is so much serious subject matter about life that society just doesn't talk about. This is why I write!

Positive and Negative Thinking

Being positive is a popular trend now! But determining what is positive or negative is left up to the beholder! Some take my writings as being negative. But I look at my writings as being positive because I'm trying to help people! If I say drugs are dangerous, that's not being negative. That's the truth! I write what I write to show people what obstacles they'll have to overcome to be successful. I write about how the world is. That's not being negative or positive. That's being a realist! I write about things I wish I had known years ago! You eventually learn in life that you have to look at the world for how it is, not how the world should be! If you go through life each day thinking how things should be, you'll never be happy! Because we're all corrupted, we're all born with sin. Don't get mad if you can't change the world! Look for things to be happy about! Be happy you can breathe air, walk, talk, and live to see another day! You cannot change other people! You cannot change other people! Even your closest family! But what you can change is YOURSELF! YOU choose what you think! YOU choose how other people effect you! YOU choose what stress you allow to effect you! YOU choose your life!

There are a lot of teachings on the "Law of Attraction." Basically that YOU attract the things that are in your life. Good or bad, and I believe this! You allow which people come into your life or stay in your life! If a man can dream it, he can achieve it! If you don't think you can do something. Guess what? That will be your result. If you don't think you're good enough to be on the football team, that will be the result. You don't think you're pretty enough to be a cheerleader, you're wish is my command. You like to brag how hard you work? Guess what? You'll be working hard the rest of your life with an attitude like that! The point is, you become what you think! If people tell you, you can't do something. Find new people to be around! Nobody supports you when you're a nobody! But every body's your best friend when you make it! So don't let other people's opinions keep you from doing what you want! Studies show that it takes 17 positive comments to counter 1 negative one. That's how powerful an impact negative thinking has on us! We dream a lot as kids. When we become adults, we're taught to stop dreaming and just go to work each day. You have hope when you dream! So get the feeling back of being a kid and believing you can do anything! Because if you believe you can't do something. That's what the universe will give you, nothing!

What I do like about the law of attraction is, that anything that's wrong with your life is your fault. And you're the only one who can fix your life! This contrasts with Christian beliefs! In Christianity, you're taught to pray about your problems and hand them over to God. But you can sit in your room all day and pray for a million dollars but God isn't going to drop it out of the sky! This is where church misleads people! Look to yourself to fix your problems! The government isn't going to fix your life! They're there to take from you! No politician, Republican or Democrat, is going to fix your life. They just want your votes! Church isn't going to fix your life, they need your money! Take action yourself! If you can't get a date, go workout in a gym! Can't get a job? Go to college!

We're programmed from birth to believe the world is a nice place and is here to help us. Only YOU can help YOU!

The law of attraction states that the universe reacts to what you think, your actual brainwaves. Even though this sounds bizarre, look at what the latest experiments in Physics tell us. Modern Physicist believe the universe is made of tiny vibrating strings, many many times smaller than an atom. Sub atomic particles inside atoms disappear and then reappear. How does this happen and where do the particles go when they leave? Physicist believe that our consciousness is what creates our reality. That the moon is in the sky because we look at it. That sub atomic particles, in lab test, react to our being there just by our consciousness. How do the sub atomic particles know we're watching them? So to say that our vibrating brainwaves interact with the universe that is made of vibrating particles, might not be so far-fetched! The law of attraction states that you tell the universe what you want and the universe rearranges itself to give you want you want. Anything's possible!

The High School Commencement Speech That Every Grad Should Read

This speech should be read at every high school graduation!!

"Congratulation students on your new high school diplomas!! You are about to enter what's called, "The Real World!"

Now I hate to bring down the mood, but 80% of what you just learned in your last 12 years of public schooling is useless information! Don't agree with me? What job can you get right now with that diploma? That's right, an entry level job making minimum wage. Public school is partly about having a place for you to go so both your parents can work and pay more taxes. Which, pays for the schools!

See.. People have been giving up their rights ever since the country started. It really started escalating after the civil war. People decided they didn't want the responsibility to educate they children anymore, let the state do it! Of course the government will gladly step in and help! But everything comes at a price! Here's the deal. We'll educate the kids in a public setting! But in return, we get to make them slaves. Because what does public school teach you? How to start a business, get a business license, how to bookkeep, billing, how to get financing, how to write expenses off your taxes, etc..?? For the most part, no. Public school teaches you how to become a good EMPLOYEE. I guess the state figures if you don't like it, then pay for your kid to go to a private school! What's the difference between public and private school? That most people come out of private school to have a good job, be a manager, or to be an entrepreneur. People from public school focus on getting a job!

An employer looking to fill a job for a bookkeeper, is looking for a person who knows how to bookkeep! The employer doesn't care if you got all A's in school, if you know how many moons Jupiter has, if you

can defragment a sentence, or solve Algebra!
These things are useless information to him!
So why doesn't the school teach bookkeeping
then? That's why you'll need to go spend 50k
on college for. And even then you'll probably
lose out to the applicant who is family or
already has bookkeeping experience! So
chances are, things aren't gonna happen
overnight! You gotta get in line with all the
others who have been waiting. So you might
as well just go party and enjoy you're youth,
because you're only young once! Why give
your youth up for something that might, or
might not, happen?!?

I want you to understand something as you
graduate today! Look around at all your
peers! You've know these people for a lot of
years! After today, you will never see about
95% of these people ever again! Even if you
see one of these people a few years down the
road at a grocery store, they're probably not
going to care to talk to you! Because life
moves on! Life is always moving forward!
Time only moves in one direction and the
past never sees the future! All the yearbooks
you have, and any other memorabilia, are
history. Most people never want to reflect on

their past! Because why reflect in the past?
The past is History! Live in the now!

Life is always changing, so always expect it to
change! You need to be selfish and live your
life for yourself! Don't live your life around
your friends. Because your friends will
eventually leave you and all you will be let
with is yourself! So put yourself and your
life's goals above hanging out with friends! A
good job, or career, is one of the most
important things in your life! Because this is
how the friend thing works; People have
friends for a reason, they need to use you for
something. The second you can't be used,
bye-bye friends! People make friends at their
job. Then when they get a new job, they leave
the old ones behind. Get used to it! Its just
how life works!

You need to understand that high school is
over and it's never coming back! I think it's a
good idea to immediately move to another
town! It doesn't have to be far! It can just be
20-30 minutes away. That way you get some
distance from your parents. You'll start
shopping at a new Walmart, Kroger, etc.. And
this helps sink in that you're grown up and on
your own. It's normal to get homesick! But

you can probably always move back if you need to! I'm just saying that if you continue to live in the town where you grew up, you'll keep that high school mentality when everybody else has moved on!

You now need to get a job or go to college. Figure out what you want to do in life and follow your dreams! You're at a point in life right now where YOU tell life what to do. YOU"RE FREE! You can do anything you want now, legally! You'll find that when you get older and get a family, LIFE starts telling you what to do. Don't waste your time with people who don't want you around! Even f it's a best friend, family, parents, etc..!! Surround yourself with people who want your company!! You can't make anybody love you! It is or it ain't! That goes for family/parents as well! You also can't change people! That's why it's important to find people who suit your needs!

And last, there is no such thing as Karma! Just look at how the rich stay rich and the poor stay poor! And if there is a God, he's not going to give you a good job, or stop you from getting in a bad car wreck, killing yourself, etc.. !! YOU are the one who has to make something happen! Explore the world! It's a big place! Sometimes you can't make things happen! Sometimes you have to let life guide you where to go! Its a tough world out here! Even the nice people are mean! Everybody's waiting to take advantage of you! Yes, even churches and Christian people! Most ministers just get into that job just so they don't have to work at McDonalds! Know when to stand your ground and when to walk away! Don't get yourself killed! Trust nobody you work with! Keep your mouth shut at work! All it can do is get you in trouble. Because tattle-taling is rewarded when you become an adult! Know rich people are just as crooked as poor people, its just they have enough money to pay the right people off! Everything in life is reversed of how you think things should be! Or reversed of what we were taught as kids! No matter how much money somebody else has or makes, they're not gonna give it to you! Yes again, even Christians! No matter how much money people make, they always spend it back on themselves!

Now after hearing this speech, you're 10 years ahead of the rest!"

Live Selfish!!

I advocate people to be selfish, at least a majority of the time! Of course there are a lot of needy people in the world who can't do for themselves and need others to do for them. I'm not against helping others at all! But... People like to tell others they're selfish and only think about themselves. Well... Aren't we all, most of us, selfish? Most of us don't spend all day in a soup kitchen working for free! Maybe, maybe, we'll do that once or twice a year. Or whatever random act of kindness. I've just found that the majority of people I've ever helped out, ended up screwing me in the end! That I took time out of my life to help someone else but when it came their turn, they just didn't feel like it. And why shouldn't we be selfish? For the most part you can't totally depend on anyone. Even your family, friends, job, etc.. These people might do some things for you. But usually when somebody does something for you, they want something in return. It's just how the world works. The people who probably do the most for you, without question, are your parents. Since it is kinda their duty to raise you, even though many parents walk out on that responsibility. Even if you have awesome parents, you still have to live your own life! You still have to follow your dreams, pursue your happiness. Because life is too short to be unhappy or to have regrets!

For example; Old people in a retirement home. Some young people feel bad for these old folks and consume their time with these old people. They're giving up their youth to give this old person company. But its not fair if this old person partied and had fun in their youth and expect a young person to give up their youth for them. Not saying you can't visit old people but don't sacrifice your life doing it! It sounds bad but it's just how the world is! This is another area where Religion fails! Because Religion teaches us not to be selfish and to give everything to others. But most people don't follow what they preach!

No matter how much money people make, they spend it back on themselves. Our society makes it sound like if we'd all pull together, we can solve all the problems. Which gives the impression to a young person that it's a caring world and somebody will help you out. Which isn't true! Nobody (maybe other than your parents) is going to help you out, you have to do it on your own! It doesn't take long to find out that the world isn't designed to give but to take from you. Ever person in every job is a sales person. Trying to sale you something you don't really need. So THEY can make money. They try to make you feel like it's about you but it's really about them. But even the liberal democrats who paint the republicans as greedy, are greedy themselves, mostly. How can you truly believe in democrat liberalism and be rich? It's oxymoronic. Just the same as a "Rich Christian." That's also oxymoronic. You can't be rich and Christian. You can't be rich and liberal. Just doesn't make sense! So just be honest and say you make a lot of money and you spend it on yourself. Instead of saying I make a lot of money and care about others. Poor people say that if they ever make a lot of money they're going to help others because they know how it feels to be poor. But in most part, when they become rich, their thinking changes. It changes to, "Well I worked hard for it! It's my money and I'm going to spend it on myself! If you want money like me, get it yourself!" So they became the very person they preached against. No matter if a person makes 50k a year or 10 million, they spend it on themself. I don't totally disagree with that but that would fit the definition of greed.

This is why some marriages don't work because one is more/less selfish than the other. You'll hardly find a relationship that's 50/50 but some are 95/5 and that's not fair to the giving person at all! I do believe in helping others! But I'd say let it take up no more than 5%-10% of your life. Spend the rest of your time doing what you want to do! Until you have kids! Once you have kids, they take priority! The same with marriage/relationships! The exception to this is any commitments you have, i.e. kids/marriage. In these cases you should fulfill what you obligated yourself to! As far as everyone else in your life, be selfish because everyone else is! Even the people who say they aren't selfish! You've got to look at people's actions, not their words! And I see most people getting up each day to serve themselves. I don't see too many waking up each day to work for free in a soup kitchen! Even rich people who give money to good causes! They do it to make themselves feel better. Cause I haven't seen one that gave all their money. And where does the money come from anyways. They take from their employees to give to someone else. So they're just taking from one person and giving it to another. Why do they give money? Why don't they work and give their time working in Africa? Cause giving money is easier! In the end, you can't control what others do! Not even your parents, kids, spouse, family, and friends. So all you ever 100% have, or can depend on, is yourself!

Bullying and How High School Never Ends!

Every person at some point in their life has had to deal with a bully. We all know the solution to a bully is to stand up and fight back. There is no talking or any other tactics that work. And all the people who are passive will just continued to get bullied. It will just get worse and worse until you solve your own problem. Violence has always been the answer in dealing with problems! It's the only language a bully will understand. Did we talk to Britain about our problems? At 1st we did but it eventually ended in war/revolution/violence. Does a cop or prison try to talk you better? No, force is used! This is a universal truth that expands all ages! For the ones who get picked on in school and think it's all going to end the day you graduate because you think grown-ups are more civilized, you're wrong! What you deal with in high school, you're going to deal with the rest of your life! Bulling, peer pressure, unfairness, etc… It's just the way it is.

People get picked on based on how fat, small, poor, race, etc, they are. So if you're naturally a big dude, then you won't have as much of this to deal with in your life. If you're a small guy, people won't hesitate to push you around! So the small guy is going to live with a disadvantage in life. My advice is get in the gym like everyone else! I believe this is one reason our founders believed in the right to bare arms. Because a 4ft tall person has no way to defend himself from a 7ft tall person, but if they both have a gun it makes them equal. People also never fight fair. Anytime a bully has something to say, he'll have 4 of his friends behind him. Another reality of life. Nobody likes to be made fun of! I find that if somebody makes fun of you, the quickest way to solve that is to turn it right back around on them. Nobodies perfect and we all have a defect. Notice a defect in the attacker, i.e their nose is big, butts big, freckles, etc.. You let the person know you ain't taking no crap and they'll move on to the next person who will take it. Now the poor kids have cyberbulling. In my day, at least if somebody got picked on, they got to go home at 3pm. Now bulling is 24 hours. But you can only be cyberbullied if you have a computer and look at it or care about it. Some kids are just destined to be picked on. Move to a new school, job, etc,.. Start a new life and reputation because you can't repair the past. If you shit your pants in 2nd grade, that will follow you your whole life! So in that case, move on to somewhere else where people don't know you, and learn from your mistakes!

Sometimes bullying leads to suicide. Well if you commit suicide you're stupid and you achieved nothing. Cause you think the people that bullied you will have to live the rest of their life with your blood on their hands. They don't care if you commit suicide. They'll just laugh about it at the next party and talked about how screwed in the head you were. You just don't have that power over other people! Worry about your own life and live for yourself. It's sad cause some are just born too good-hearted in a heartless tough world! And sometimes standing up for yourself can get you killed. You have to access each situation of what the smartest thing to do is. Sometimes it's the smartest decision to walk away. I'm more for standing up for yourself if it's in a day to day situation like school, work, etc.. If its a random situation like road rage. Who cares, just walk away! Or in that case drive away.

Our society teaches us to not fight and be docile. That's just another way for the people at the top to suppress the ones at the bottom. Cause they'll tell you not to fight but they'll fight and stand up for themselves.

The school caters to the jocks and hot chics, this also never changes in life. Our society caters to the football player, cheerleader, etc.. Our society likes to see these people succeed and doesn't care about the fat and ugly. Stick them in the corner with all the other problems of the world because society doesn't want these people ruining their good time! It looks like it's really evolution in action, the survival of the fittest.

This is why you have to have friends! When you're alone, people will mess with you! The same people won't mess with you when you're in a group. Which means everyone has to join a type of gang or click. Once again, we're taught that gangs are wrong. But you have to be in one to stay safe!

To Succeed in Business, You Must Be a Good Liar!!

Perception is Reality!

There are two reality's. The real you, and the way people perceive you. Which is along

the lines of being a con-artist. For example;
in your secret personal life, you could be a
drug dealer/user or whatever other sin you
can think of. But to everyone else you act like
a good Christian person. So everybody
including family, friends, coworkers, spouse,
kids, and the general public think you are a
person you're not. So which one is reality?
Both are. Most everybody acts this way in
public! You hardly find a genuine person.
Because we all try to act like a person others
will like. Which in itself is lying or living a lie.
Yes, even for the church going Christians.
Usually people are the most genuine with their
spouse, kids, and family! So basically we're all
con-artist! We're all conning people every
time we walk out the door! Just some do it
more than others and some do it better than
others! We are supposed to judge people on
their actions but for the most part we don't.
For our society, people can do whatever sin
they want as long as they talk good and tell
others what they want to hear! Very sad!!

I'm not an advocate for lying and living a
fake life! But when it comes to working a job,
you have to!! We claim to be a nation built on
individuals and individual thought. But when
you go to work, employers don't want

individuals! They want a like-minded group of obedient slaves who can do a job faster and cheaper than the competition! So they, the employer/boss, can go out shopping all day or hang out at the golf course during business hours. But the employees can't live a life like that! They didn't "earn" it! That life is only for the elite! So you have to go to work, lie all day, and be the fake person they pay you to be! Cause business doesn't always reward telling the truth! They say that honesty is the best policy but I've seen people get fired over telling the truth! Now honesty is the best policy in your personal life with your family or if you're under oath! Your employer/boss will lie to you like its nothing, so why should it not be that way in reverse? For some reason work can't be as simple as if you do your job or not. It also depends on if others like you or not. Cause every person you work with is your boss! Cause work encourages people to tattle on each other, and the boss likes tattletales so he doesn't have to do his job. So even though we're taught to "be ourselves" and that people should "like us for who we are." In reality you have to go to work, bite your tongue, and act like somebody else. To succeed in business, you must be a good liar!!

In Closing

What do you want to happen when you die? What if you have small kids? Who do you want them to learn from? In a perfect world we would all raise our kids until old age, but not everyone gets that option. That's why I ask the question of who do you want your kids to learn from. This information is as important as having a will! I hope you have enjoyed reading! Tell your friends!

If you like this book, check out my other books!

"A Secret Lie: How The World Really Is:"
http://www.amazon.com/dp/B007P5CJKM

"CREATE Your Way Out Of DEBT"
http://www.amazon.com/dp/B00LGX57J4

"How Ta Get PU$$Y"
http://www.amazon.com/dp/B00L0LZC6U

Check out my newest film about how the world really is:

https://www.createspace.com/403985

Check out my NEW Audiobooks for FREE at:

on Relationships:
http://open.spotify.com/album/64vuXdOD VyppQcsrX807M5

on Religion:
http://open.spotify.com/album/0SY2Wtr5jn UouXGeboSVNO

Like to Laugh? Click this link to see the funniest, just released, stand-up comedy FREE!

http://open.spotify.com/album/2S65s3bo HGcsDzZIUwy8aO

For the Best Alternative Rock Music, click below!

http://open.spotify.com/album/7A1p0qBw

3oov8bKYsA26Aw